Published in Nashville, Tennessee, by Tommy Nelson®
a division of Thomas Nelson, Inc.
Publisher: Laura Minchew
Production Manager: Karen Gallini

Designed by Gregory Rohm
Koechel Peterson & Associates

Library of Congress Cataloging-in-Publication Data

Mackall, Dandi Daley.
  Joseph, king of dreams / adapted by Dandi Daley Mackall. — Classic ed.
    p. cm.
  ISBN 0-8499-7693-6
  1. Joseph (Son of Jacob)—Juvenile literature. [1. Joseph (Son of Jacob) 2. Bible
stories--O.T.] I. Title.

BS580.J6 .M33 2000
222'.1109505--dc21

00-058404

Printed in the United States of America
00 01 02 03 04 PHX 9 8 7 6 5 4 3 2 1

JOSEPH
KING OF DREAMS

Adapted by Dandi Daley Mackall

DREAMWORKS.

Tommy
NELSON
Thomas Nelson, Inc.
Nashville

On a starry night many years ago in the land of Canaan, a miraculous event came to pass. Jacob deeply loved his wife Rachel and thought she could never have children. But, to their joy and delight, Rachel was finally having a baby. And although he already had ten sons, Jacob celebrated the birth of baby Joseph above all others.

"Oh, God," Jacob prayed, "you have blessed me with a gift beyond measure, a miracle, a treasure."

While Judah, Simeon, Reuben, and the other brothers worked in the fields, Jacob and Rachel delighted in Joseph. But as the favorite son grew he also became the least favored brother.

One day Jacob and Rachel gave Joseph a coat of many colors as bright as butterflies. Burning with jealousy, his brothers watched as Joseph proudly slipped his arms into the long sleeves and admired his reflection in the well.

Joseph had many dreams, dreams that miraculously came to pass. One night he had an extraordinary vision.

"Not another dream," Issachar complained.

"This time my dream was about all of you," Joseph said. "We were carrying sheaves of wheat, and all of a sudden I was above you and your wheat bowed down to me."

"I wonder what *that's* supposed to mean?" Levi snapped.

"Next," Joseph continued dramatically, "the stars were bowing to me, too!"

"God may be telling us something of our future," Jacob told his sons.

"Judah has led the herd for years! He comes first before any of us," Simeon spat out the words.

"I've had enough of this!" Judah shouted, storming off.

"I didn't ask for the dream," Joseph said.

Simeon elbowed him in the stomach as he brushed past. "You didn't ask for that either, brother."

Joseph doubled over from the blow. "*Half* brother," he muttered.

Rachel calmed Joseph and tried to help him understand his brothers' feelings.

Not long after, Joseph went in search of his brothers, who were already plotting against *the dreamer*. They lay in wait, seized Joseph, and pulled off his many-colored coat.

"Are you going to tell on us?" Simeon shouted, tossing the coat to Issachar, who threw it to Judah.

"That's *my* coat!" Joseph yelled in horror as his brothers ripped his treasured coat.

His brothers closed in on him, and backed him to the edge of a deep pit, where he fell in.

"Help!" Joseph yelled as he landed with a thud and a cloud of dust. From the depths of the parched hole, he cried out, "Somebody!" But above him, voices drifted farther away.

Joseph huddled against the rough dirt walls as darkness fell. Something crawled onto his shoulder, and he turned to see a scorpion. Frustrated, Joseph flung it to the ground and screamed for his brothers. "Please! Don't leave me here alone!"

After hours shivering under the cold moonlight, Joseph saw a rope dropped into the pit. "Finally!" he shouted, climbing up. "Father won't think this is so funny when he hears—"

But Joseph was surprised that his rescuers were Ishmaelite traders. "My brothers will come for me!" he threatened. And they did—but, only to collect their payment for Joseph. "As agreed, twenty

pieces of silver," said one trader, tossing a coin bag to Judah.

With horror, Joseph finally understood. His brothers were actually selling him into slavery.

Joseph's brothers ignored his cries as the traders bound his hands and dragged him away.

Then, the brothers killed a goat and dipped Joseph's coat in its blood. They led their parents to believe that a wild animal had killed Joseph.

The caravan wound across miles of desert on its way to the land of Egypt. Stumbling behind a camel, Joseph passed endless days in hot shifting sands, followed by cold cruel nights and the torments of even crueler traders. He tried not to think of all he was leaving behind . . . or all that lay ahead.

At last the dust cleared, and Joseph saw distant buildings of stone stretching toward the heavens. He had longed to see the wonders of Egypt, but never like this.

They entered the city through noisy streets, where the wealthy strutted in gold and silks. Egyptian women called out prices as they bought and sold glittering jewels.

At the docks, Joseph watched as animals and people were hauled to the auction block. A crude sign was slipped around his neck, and Joseph was yanked into line with the other slaves.

A well-dressed Egyptian servant frowned as he examined Joseph. "My master Potiphar, captain of Pharaoh's guard, needs a household slave. This Canaanite will do." And just like that, Joseph was sold again.

At Potiphar's palace, Joseph worked as hard as he had seen his brothers work. How could they have done this to me? he wondered.

Yet Joseph obediently completed every task assigned. Soon even Potiphar and his wife, Zuleika, noticed the hard-working Canaanite slave. Eventually, they brought Joseph into the palace to serve in their banquet hall.

Zuleika loved
nothing more than hosting
lavish parties. As Joseph rushed
around the banquet room, seeing
to preparations, a cat scrambled
across the table and sprang to a high
beam. Only Joseph was able to
coax it down.

"My cat seems to like you," said
a sweet voice. "I am Asenath."

Joseph turned to see an amazing girl. He handed her the cat. And as they talked, Joseph began to fall in love.

As the years passed, Joseph faithfully looked after his master's interests, even protecting him from dishonest tradesmen. When Potiphar saw that Joseph was successful in everything he did, he appointed Joseph as overseer. And under Joseph's care, Potiphar's palace flourished.

Although Joseph still missed his homeland, his Egyptian life had begun to bring its own rewards. But those rewards were not to last.

Day after day, Zuleika observed Joseph, now strong and handsome. One night she secretly came to Joseph and asked him to betray Potiphar's trust.

But Joseph refused and tried to leave.

"I order you to stay!" she shouted, grabbing him.

Joseph ran off down the hall, leaving his torn shirt in her fist. Behind him, a cry rose, filling the palace. "Help! The slave attacked me!"

The guards arrested Joseph and took him to
Potiphar, who flew into a rage at his wife's words.

"I gave you my trust!" he bellowed at Joseph.

"I swear, I did nothing to betray you,"
Joseph insisted.

"Silence!" Potiphar shouted, holding up as
evidence the torn shirt. "Take him to prison."

"Please believe me. I did nothing wrong!" Joseph
cried as guards dragged him to a dark, rat-infested
cell and slammed the door.

One morning, two of Joseph's fellow prisoners awoke from disturbing dreams. "I saw a vine with three branches," said the cupbearer. "I squeezed the grapes from the vine into a cup for Pharaoh."

"In three days Pharaoh will bring you back to the palace a free man," Joseph explained happily.

Pharaoh's baker went next. "I dreamed three bread baskets sat on my head, and from out of nowhere birds attacked."

Sadly, Joseph explained: "Your dream means that in three days, Pharaoh will put you to death."

Three days later guards stormed the prison, taking the baker off for execution and the cupbearer back to the palace. "Tell Pharaoh about me!" Joseph called after the cupbearer. "Don't forget me!"

But the cupbearer did forget, and Joseph suffered in prison day after day. Sold into slavery by his own brothers, and now thrown into prison for a crime he had not committed, Joseph cried out to God, "Why are you doing this to me? Why?" Enraged, he stomped on a small plant growing in the prison floor.

The next morning Joseph woke to a shaft of light streaming down through the prison bars. He gazed up at a patch of clear, blue sky and felt a glimmer of hope. In the middle of his cell, a tiny leaf still grew from the trampled tree. Joseph watered the young plant with care, slowly realizing that God was caring for him, too. God hadn't forgotten him or the fragile tree. And even if Joseph could not understand why he was in a prison in Egypt, he knew God must have a plan for him.

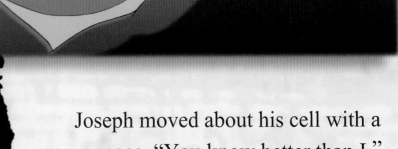

Joseph moved about his cell with a new peace. "You know better than I," he sang to God, his constant companion.

Years passed, and Joseph transformed himself and his surroundings. When at last the cell door opened, Joseph was surprised to see Potiphar.

"Pharaoh is tortured by a dream. None of his wise men can explain it. I'm to bring you to the palace," Potiphar said, with difficulty.

"Potiphar, I understand. I forgive you," said Joseph.

Joseph took one last look at the tree that had sprung from an abandoned seed. Now thirty years old, Joseph knew that he, too, had grown in prison.

Joseph was brought to a grand palace, where a tormented man knelt before an altar. The man rose, put on his Egyptian headdress, and Joseph stood before Pharaoh, the king of all Egypt. "They tell me you can interpret dreams," said Pharaoh.

"Not me, Your Excellency," Joseph replied. "The explanation comes from God. Tell me your dream, Pharaoh."

Pharaoh trembled as he related his dream to Joseph: "Seven healthy cows graze peacefully on the banks of the Nile. Then seven sickly cows come out of the river and devour them."

Joseph waited until Pharaoh revealed his second dream, in which seven full heads of grain were swallowed by seven shriveled and scorched ones.

"Well?" Pharaoh demanded, challenging Joseph to do what none of his magicians or their gods could. "Tell me the meaning!"

Joseph spoke with confidence: "Egypt will have seven years of abundance, followed by seven years of famine. You must choose someone to collect one-fifth of the grain during the seven years of plenty and store it for the seven years of famine."

Pharaoh trusted Joseph's interpretation. He appointed Joseph over all Egypt and presented him to the crowd. As the people cheered, Joseph looked to heaven and praised God.

Joseph took Asenath as his wife, for their love had endured his years in prison. For the next seven years, the entire land of Egypt prospered under Joseph's leadership. Workers pulled together, harvesting abundant crops. And Joseph and Asenath celebrated the birth of their two sons.

Joseph supervised the building of huge grain storehouses that stretched into the skies. Workers carried sacks of grain up spiraling steps and filled the enormous silos.

Joseph traveled throughout Egypt, overseeing the collection of one-fifth of every harvest. As the seven years of good crops drew to an end, Joseph sensed in the howling wind the fulfillment of Pharaoh's dream. And he braced for what he knew was yet to come.

Before Egyptian eyes, crops turned to dry brush, and animal carcasses littered the once fertile ground. Starving people came from all across the land for grain from Joseph's silos. He passed out the stored grain fairly, ensuring that no man, woman, or child would suffer starvation in Egypt.

But hunger spread beyond Egypt, all the way to the once fertile valleys of Canaan. And so it was that one day as Joseph handed out the apportioned grain, he heard a familiar voice and turned to see his own brothers. Twenty years had passed, but Joseph had no difficulty recognizing the brothers who had sold him into slavery.

"**M**y brothers and I have traveled from Canaan to buy food for our hungry families," Judah explained. None of the brothers recognized Joseph.

Joseph's heart froze at the memory of all he had endured at their hands. "Spies!" he shouted. "Are you thieves hoping to steal our grain? Throw them in prison!"

"Excellency," Judah begged, "we are simply ten brothers, with a younger brother and old father at home."

Surprised to hear of a younger brother, Joseph demanded, "Then prove it! Produce this youngest brother." And to guarantee their return, he held one of them—Simeon—in prison.

Later, Joseph broke down and confided to his wife that these men were his brothers, who had sold him into slavery. "I thought you had learned something in that cell," Asenath said sadly.

When at last Joseph was told that the Canaanites had returned, he donned his Egyptian garb and invited them to dine with him. Joseph couldn't keep his eyes off his brother Benjamin, who looked so much like himself at that age . . . before his brothers betrayed him.

Benjamin told Joseph of their father, and of the brother who was killed by wolves. Joseph could barely control his anger. He glanced at his brothers, who looked away in shame for having lied to Benjamin all his life.

As Joseph watched his brothers dine, he conceived a plot to entrap them. He instructed his servant to fill the brothers' bags with grain, returning their silver, and secretly place his royal cup in Benjamin's sack. The next day, he had his brothers arrested for thievery. The grain sacks were sliced open, and the "stolen" cup was discovered in Benjamin's sack.

"This is how you repay my kindness? By stealing? Arrest him!" Joseph ordered the palace guards.

"I didn't take your cup!" Benjamin cried.

The other brothers protested, and Judah stepped forward, bowing to Joseph. "Stop! Take me instead. I beg you."

"You would sacrifice yourselves for a half brother who's spoiled by your father?" Joseph asked. "Why should you care if I make him my slave?"

"Because," Judah answered, "I will not make my father suffer . . . again." Then Judah confessed the guilt they had lived with for twenty years. "Our brother was not killed by wolves. We were blinded by jealousy and sold him into slavery. My father could not bear such loss a second time. And neither could we. If anyone is to be punished, it should be us."

Joseph stared at his brothers. They were willing to exchange their own lives for the life of their father's favorite? They had changed, just as Joseph had changed.

Overcome, Joseph flung his arms around Judah. "I will not harm any of you . . . or our father. I am your brother Joseph."

35

Astounded, Simeon stepped closer. "How can it be?"

"Joseph?" Judah asked. "Can you ever forgive us?"

Joseph embraced his brothers and wept. "I already have. Can you forgive me for thinking I was some miracle—"

"But you *are* a miracle!" Judah insisted. "God sent you to save our family and all of Egypt."

Then Joseph introduced his brothers to his wife and sons, and there was great rejoicing. And his brothers returned home to bring their father and families to Egypt.

Joseph and Asenath waited with their sons on the outskirts of Egypt. "Here they come!" cried their oldest son.

A caravan wound its way across the desert. Then Joseph caught sight of his aged father, bent like the acacia tree of his homeland. "Father!" he shouted, racing down the hill and into his father's arms.

"Joseph," Jacob cried. "My son! It's a miracle."

37

Jacob's family lived happily in the land of Goshen in Egypt. Joseph continued to grow in wisdom and favor with God. And as the years went by, Jacob's children and grandchildren and their children multiplied in numbers and strength. The stories were told from generation to generation of how God chose Joseph to build a great nation because he was faithful and willing to forgive.